Table of Contents

About the Author 2
Introduction: Becoming A Distributed Business 3
Process and Routine 5
Project Management Tools 10
Chat and Messaging apps 18
Video Conferencing and Screen Sharing 22
Video / Screen Recording & Screen Capture 27
Collaborative Documents 31
Drive Sharing 37
Wiki 40
Password Management 43
Time Tracking 46
Reporting 50
Document Tracking / Electronic Agreements 52
Health and Wellbeing 55
Final Words 59

About the Author

Mark has a degree in Psychology and an MBA. He has spent over a decade working in the field of digital marketing. In that time he has built a marketing agency which today is largely run remotely. The agency consists of 14 staff and services over 40 clients in Australia and around the world.

Mark has a keen interest in business and project management which includes developing efficient and practical ways of running remote teams. He also has strong interest in marketing strategy and machine learning.

Mark has written widely about these topics on major industry publications and created 3 best selling Udemy courses for marketers.

Introduction: Becoming A Distributed Business

Many businesses are looking to offer flexibility to their staff by providing work from home options. There are many considerations for managers running remote teams and fortunately there are many processes and tools already in the market to support distributed businesses. Members of our team have been working remotely already for years and we are in a position to share our knowledge on how we maximize productivity and wellbeing through our processes. In this guide I'll take you through the processes that work well for us and review the best tools to keep you running efficiently.

We are a digital marketing agency with 6 core staff in the office and another 8 staff working remotely all over the world. We have team members in Australia, England, the US, Bali, South Africa, Spain, China and Eastern Europe. Remote working has become part of our DNA and it means we can take advantage of expertise all around the world. Many businesses when making the transition to working with remote staff think they may be able to continue working as normal. But the truth is that running a remote team is a different game and in order to make it work well and efficiently there are many aspects in the day to day running of a business that have to adapt to suit remote working as we will discuss.

There are certain advantages to working remotely, the tools we have in place allow us to be extremely efficient internally, ensure we remain up to date, maximize collaboration and deliver strong client transparency and support. We've learnt that the tools we are forced to use to run a remote team will also benefit a local team.

The following guide covers key items you need to know in running a team remotely and how to squeeze the most out of working remotely. The guide is divided into 12 sections, within each section we look at the best tools in our experience and why you should use them.

Process and Routine

Having a daily routine is important no matter who you are and what you do. For teams working remotely and isolated from each other it is even more crucial. It is easy for staff to feel isolated, come off track or lose motivation when they are away from the rest of their team. Having a routine allows team members to sync up daily and ensure they stay on track and feel part of the larger team.

The Daily Scrum

The daily standup or 'scrum' is a very important routine to implement within remote teams. This concept comes from Agile project management, which is used mainly by software development teams, but can easily be adapted. The core idea is to dedicate a time, near the beginning of the day where all team members meet for a short period (about 15 to 20 mins). This should be a quick catch up. It's OK to chit chat a bit and talk about daily events or something funny that happened, but it should mostly be kept short and efficient. In our team we ask each member of the team to outline key tasks they are working on today (not everything and every detail). The idea is to bring out any issues they are having or anything that is blocking them in getting their tasks done. Atlassian has some great suggestions around [how to run the daily scrum](). (keep in mind it is geared towards software developers, you should adapt it to your team)

The daily scrum is the key meeting of the day, it's important to pull the team together, ensure everyone is on track and is aware of what work is being done by the team. You will be surprised how much interaction happens between team members you didn't realize needed to happen. The scrum facilitates this.

Segmenting Your Day

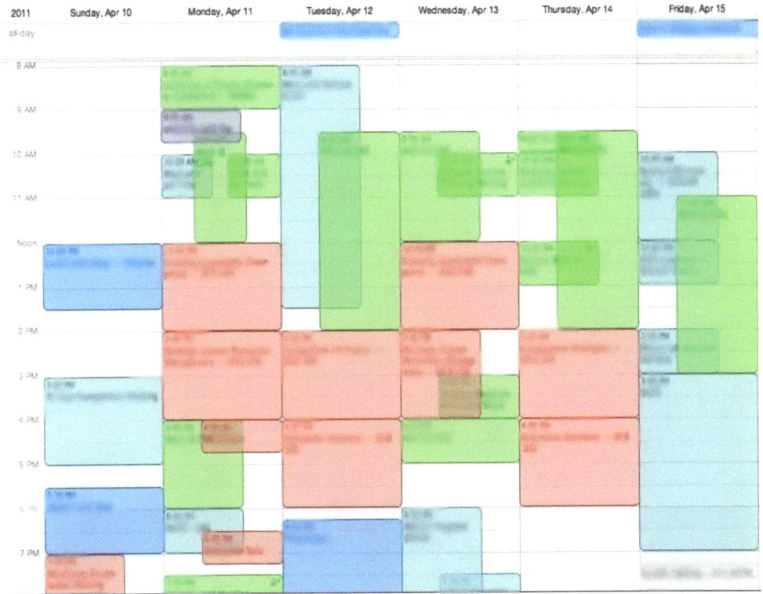

It's also important to schedule in other team meetings during the day using digital calendars such as outlook or Google Calendar. For example, we have a bi-weekly sales meeting, where we review items in our CRM together on Zoom conferencing and discuss the progress of each lead.

Segmenting your day is a critical aspect to regular work and remote work. The nature of the day has a tendency to throw things at you. If you work through your day constantly responding to your environment, rather than controlling your own day, the day ends up controlling you. Taking control of your day requires you to allocate times for different things. This is how you manage your time better.

For example, looking at your day you can see that you are going to spend 1 hour in internal meetings, 1 hour in client meetings, this gives you another 6 hours which you can allocate between responding to emails, working on deliverables and whatever else needs to get done. At the beginning of your day, you should allocate time to each of these tasks. If you have scheduled time, this allows you to manage the time better.

Prioritize Deep Creative Work Early

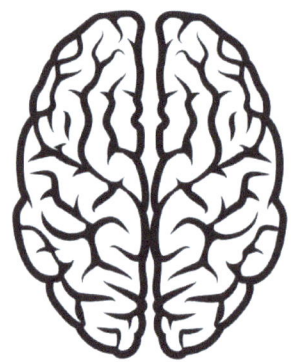

Limits on our creative focus should be taken into account when allocating your daily routine. Studies have shown that we only have about two hours of real creative work during the day. A survey conducted in the 1950's shows that productivity peaks at around 10 to 20 hours per week. There are many examples of famous scientists and writers like Charles Darwin that were known for spending only 4 hours in the morning working and the rest of their day on leisurely activities. See Alex Soojung-Kim Pang's book 'Rest' where he brings a number of high profile examples of people that were able to be immensely productive and creative in limited amounts of time, ultimately changing the world.

For most of us, the start of the day is when our brain's are the freshest and working the best. Once these hours are used up, your creative energies weaken. Considering that you only have around 2 hours of *real creative work* you want to use this time on tasks that are most important to you and your business. For me this is working on critical deliverables for a client, or new content or coming up with creative strategy for the business. I try and fit this into the morning hours of my day and move meetings later in the day. Having a quiet couple of hours in the morning is critical to getting key work done.

Project Management Tools

In my opinion, the most critical component of running a remote team is selecting the right project management philosophy and tools. The right project management tool will tie aspects of your project and team together and integrate other tools. When done right, your project management tool becomes your central work hub.   Since projects are often varied and have multiple components and variables it is critical to choose the right tool that will assist your business and increase flexibility.

The market is saturated with 100's of project management tools. Many are similar and they all copy some aspects of each other. We have used a number of the biggest players in the field including:

- Basecamp
- Asana
- Trello
- Jira
- Monday
- ClickUp
- Streak

For our business requirements, the tool that consistently came out on top was ClickUp. There are 5 key aspects that were critical for us and will likely be the same for you, I'll take you through them and why ClickUp became our project management tool of choice.

1) Flexibility

Many project management tools are built for a specific project type and when you try and use it for another project it does not meet the needs. Projects are dynamic, they change. As an agency we manage multiple projects, all of them have different stages, requirements, and goals. ClickUp has an extremely flexible hierarchical structure that can adapt to different project types. ClickUp starts with a high level project space. Within that space are folders. Each folder contains lists and the individual tasks sit within these lists.

In our businesses we've customized this for our purposes. A project space for examples is everything One Egg does (box 1 in the screenshot below). Another space could be a side project we are working on. Within the One Egg space, each folder is a client (box 2 shows OED as a client). For each client, we have multiple lists. One is Content (Box 3), another is Social Media, and so on, covering all the projects that we are working on for OED clients.

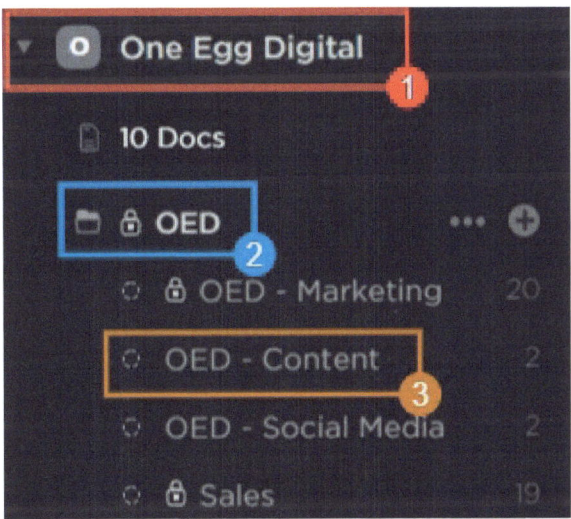

Within those lists fall all the tasks we are working on. Each project list can have different stages depending on the requirement of the project. We can also assign tasks to multiple owners, we can have subtasks and dependent tasks. 2 examples of tasks can be seen below

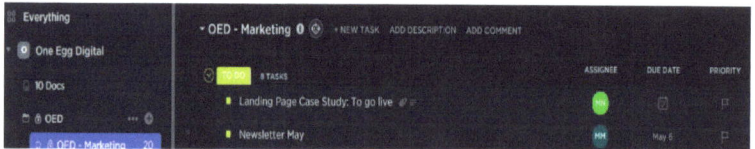

One of our core tenants as an agency is transparency. ClickUp's flexibility lets us have control over privacy and who can see which tasks. We can bring in clients as guests to view and comment on certain tasks and projects but not others. We can also ensure that staff members are only working on projects relevant to them..

2) Ease of use

There are some tools that have amazing features but are difficult to use. This may work for you individually since you have invested in learning the tool, but getting your team and your clients to use it will be more challenging if the learning curve is too high. Not everyone may be as tech savvy as you and the tools will only work well if everyone is on board. It should be intuitive to use from the outset so that it can grow with your team. It should also have good documentation and a strong supporting team behind it.

We found ClickUp to be fairly straightforward to use. It is extremely flexible, it does have more options and customizations then some other project management tools, which makes it slightly more of a learning curve. [Asana](#), for example, is easier to use out of the box, but has less customization power. Where ClickUp shines especially, is in the support and documentation provided.

There are constant updates and thorough and easily accessible supporting information.

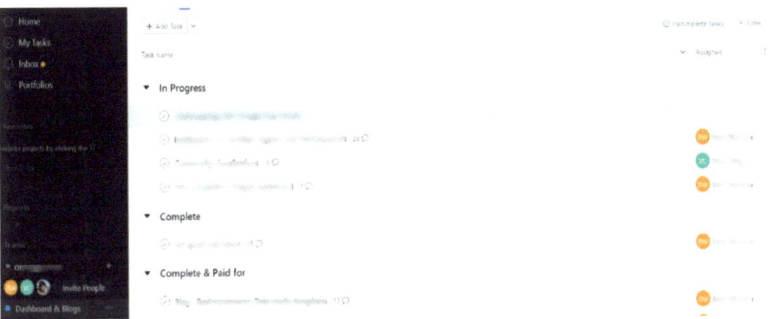

Image: The Asana interface is clean, has a short learning curve, but offers less customization

3) Communication

We've dedicated a section further on to talk in more depth about communication tools like Slack. Yet it's surprising how a great project management tool can handle a lot of your team communication needs. The transition to a project management tool will transport your communication about a specific task out of email and into a task based system. Email is a messy way to run a project, it isn't designed for it, yet so many companies still do it this way because it is the default. Project management tools are centered around tasks and designed to focus communication on each task. It is a change of mindset and discipline to move away from emails and into a project management tool, but it is far more organized.

Most project management tools facilitate this well with the ability to comment and have running discussions on tasks. Users can be tagged in discussion to ensure they receive notifications (via email) on new comments directed or assigned to them. Below is a screenshot of the commentary section in ClickUp showing a three-way discussion with users tagged.

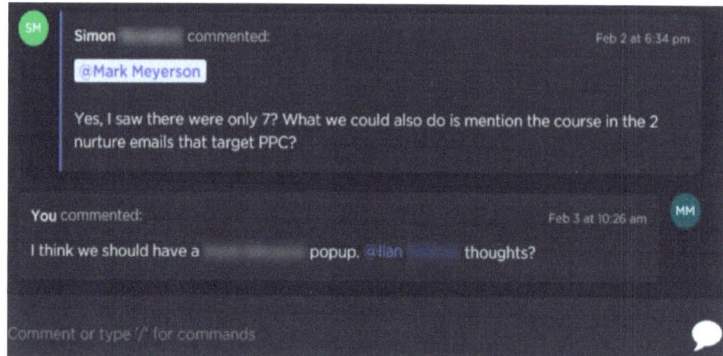

The ability to also assign tasks is a key aspect of project management. ClickUp for example allows you to assign tasks to multiple users.

A number of project management tools like ClickUp & Monday.com have also integrated video collaboration into the task screen. This allows you to conveniently start a conference call with members of your current task.

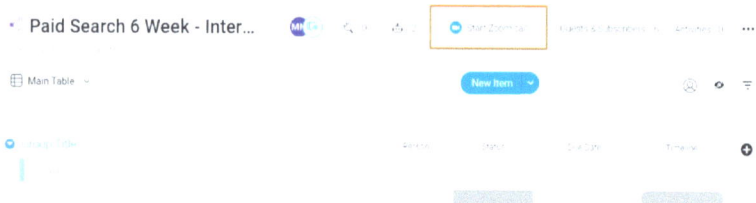

Screenshot of task screen from Monday.com, showing 'Start Zoom Call' Button

We discussed how these tools allow you to move communication into them. However it's undeniable that most communication still happens in email and making that leap can be a challenge. When it comes to solving email integration, the best project management tool I have used is [Streak](). The brilliance of streak is that it actually sits within your Gmail account as an add-on. Originally designed as a CRM, it works just as well as a project management tool. The basic idea in Streak is to create boxes which you can think of as 'tasks' and then assign emails to those boxes. Within your box you can include data related to a project, such as description, assignee, notes or any other custom field. Practically speaking, when I receive an email from a client related to a task, I can easily assign the email to the task (or create a new task). Then I send off a new email to someone in my team and assign the task to them. All of this information including all emails, assignees and task notes is linked through the one box. For interested readers I have written an [in depth review of how you can use Streak as a project management tool.]()

With Streak there's no need to open a 3rd party project management application. As you can see in the screenshot below, with Streak we have multiple pipelines (task lists) in the sidebar (box 1) and then the main screen we sort each of our boxes according to stages, such as 'in progress' and 'completed'. All this is within Gmail.

Streak is a fantastic product if you are a freelancer managing the communication yourself. But once you bring in other team members it can be more challenging because there is a steep learning curve, it's expensive per user and it is missing many other important features that other project management tools have.

4) Time Tracking & Reporting

A great project management tool should pull all aspects of your work flow together. It should help you organize everything in one place and drive efficiency. Ultimately becoming your go to tool and your springboard for all other work. Some tools like ClickUp allow you to track project time and report on progress easily in one place.

There are some great time tracking tools out there which we will discuss further on. But ideally team time tracking should be done against your projects in your tool. ClickUp allows you to create time estimates for each task and then track actual time against these tasks.

ClickUp also provides dashboards to review how projects are tracking, how team members are progressing on tasks and which projects are falling behind and becoming overdue. There are reports detailing estimated vs actual time per task and project group. Below is an example of a ClickUp dashboard with scoring for each team member based on task interaction and completion.

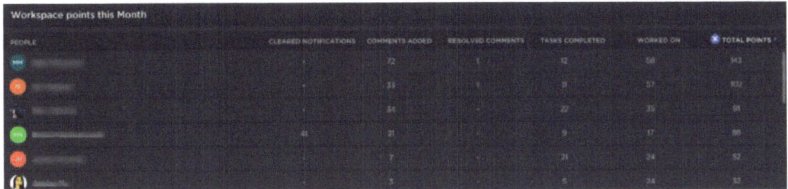

5) Growth Potential

Your project management tool needs to be flexible, easy to use and provide strong communication and reporting. Without these aspects the tool will not grow with your team. Another no less important consideration is pricing. The tool needs to have the right balance of features and pricing. Consider your growing team as well as guest contractors and clients that need access to the tool, as you grow user based pricing can become an issue. ClickUp is the most reasonable tool we have found from this aspect. This is why we recommend it overall.

Chat and Messaging apps

Social networking in the workplace happens naturally every day when you work in a physical office with your colleagues. The importance of these interactions to the health and performance of employees and the business overall cannot be understated. People naturally discuss social issues, life events and aspects of their work interchangeably in the flow of conversation. It takes time for colleagues to get to know each other through conversation and experience and feel comfortable working together. Employees that feel more comfortable with each other will tend to work better together as a team. This is referred to as social capital, a reference to the value of the relationships and networks that employees build with each other.

The Importance of Social Interaction in the Workplace

Several studies illustrate the importance of social interaction in the workplace. Sozbilir, found that social capital has an effect on organizational creativity and organizational efficiency. Hudaykulov & Hongyi showed that findings suggest there is a large positive impact of social capital on cooperation.

If you are running a remote team it is critical to facilitate interactions between team members. Regular scheduled meetings as already discussed above are an important component. Communication on email and/or in a project management tool is different to chat because it is tightly structured around tasks. In most cases you don't want to see unrelated comments and general social chat within email or project management comments. This is why it's important to facilitate a chat based app.

Slack

[Slack](#) is the tool of choice for chat for most companies. Slack is a messaging app which allows your whole team to communicate. It uses "Channels" which are like chat rooms that are designated for specific discussions. A Channel could be set up for a project or a team or a client, where all discussion for relevant team members is based around that item. Channels can also be set up a company wide discussion forum, or a social forum, or anything of the like. Aside from channels It is also possible to direct message users on the platform for one on one discussions.

I've outlined in the screenshot below how you can access channels (box 1) and direct messages (box 2) in slack

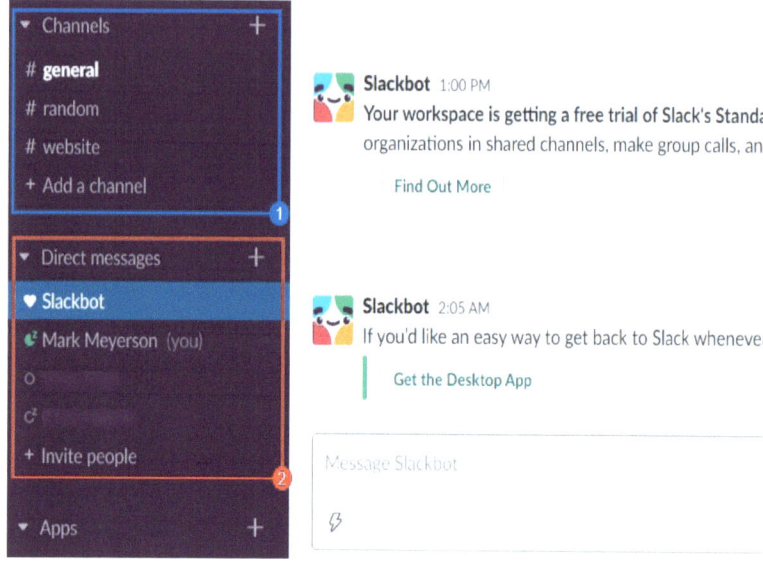

Slack has a number of advantages. It's extremely user friendly, you can just hop on and intuitively work with it immediately. It's widely used and it's likely that your clients or contractors are using it already, so you can easily pull them into your projects and take advantage of the network effects. It integrates well and widely with other tools allowing you to set up notifications and pull information from other tools like your CMS into your slack channels.

Slack Alternatives

There are alternatives to slack that are free. We used Facebook Workplace Chat for some time but we didn't like it. We thought that since it was structured like Facebook our team would gravitate towards it and use it like an internal social network. However this didn't happen and it was not very user friendly. We are now using Google Chat, which we are finding far better. It doesn't have all the features that Slack has, but it is free, low frills and does everything we need including the ability to create channels. We also love that it integrates into Gmail, it can be used as a standalone app but also from within your Gmail account. We can access Google Chats from within Gmail and all chats are searchable in Gmail. In order to use Google Chat you need to be using G Suite.

In the screenshot below you can see how chat boxes sit at the bottom of the screen within my Gmail app and I can actively chat with colleagues while working in email. Each one of those boxes is a conversation between myself and a colleague or client. This can be extremely useful for clarifying emails.

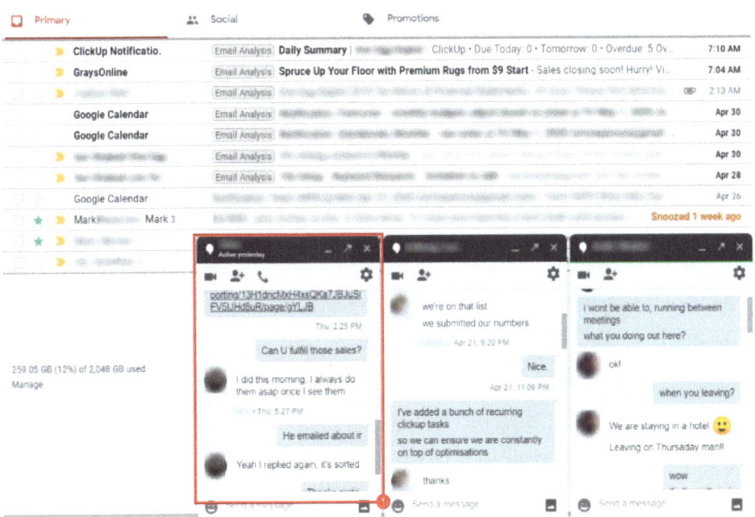

Skype is another well known chat application. It was widely used as one of the first video and messaging apps. Lately it has fallen behind other applications and fallen from popularity.

Video Conferencing and Screen Sharing

Zoom Video Conference Interface

Video conferencing is crucial for remote teams to facilitate both client and internal communication. It's important to ensure your team is on the same platform and regularly using video conferencing. As discussed above, having regular interactions within your team is more important than we often realize and video chat among other forms of communication must be facilitated for a healthy and productive team.

Popular Video Conferencing Solutions

The most popular solutions today are: Zoom, Google Hangouts, Microsoft Teams, Skype, GotoMeetings &

BlueJeans. I've used all of the above and they are all fairly similar. The key features that you want in your video conferencing software are:

- Ability to have multiple team members join a meeting by video. Most of them allow at least 25 or more for free.
- Join via link - Access these meetings on your phone or PC with a link that can be shared via email or messaging.
- Screen Sharing
- Chat
- Ability to mute / turn off screen
- Record meeting

All of the aforementioned tools allow for capabilities listed above and they are all fairly similar. All of these key players also all have similar levels of quality in air time. Essentially there are two main considerations: price and security.

Security Considerations

Zoom has recently come under scrutiny for security issues and are being investigated for misleading claims. It's worth considering these issues before using the app. These are outlined in detail here (but are likely to change by the time you are reading this article). Also consider that Zoom provides video conferencing for free but only up to 40 minutes which can be extremely frustrating, especially on a sales call!

Google Hangouts

At One Egg, we've been using Google Hangouts. The best thing about Google Hangouts is that it is free. The second best thing, relevant mainly if you work in the Google ecosystem, is that it integrates seamlessly with other Google tools like Email, Chat, Google Calendar. When I create a calendar meeting, Google Calendar automatically creates a Google Hangout room with a link, the video conference 'hangout' is automatically set up & all meeting attendees automatically invited. The same with chat, while in the midst of a chat, I can move seamlessly into a video conference with one click. This is extremely convenient. The below screenshot shows how the Google hangout link is automatically created when adding a new meeting in Google Calendar.

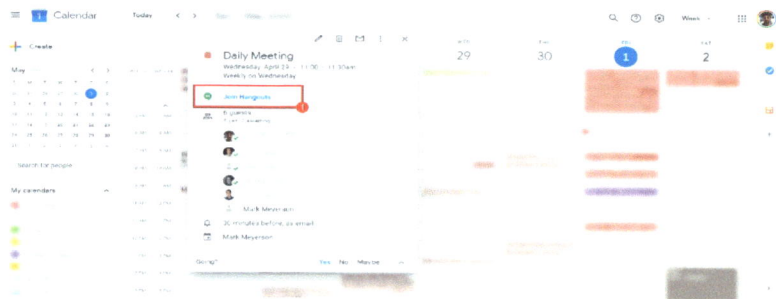

Screen Sharing

Screen Sharing in Google Hangouts

Screen Sharing is a key feature that these video conferencing software products offer. This is the ability for one person on the inside of a video conference to share their active computer screen to the other members on the call in real time. This is an extremely useful and underrated feature that we use all the time.

The applications of this are many. In internal team meetings there have been countless times that a team member is explaining an issue which is hard to visualize and another member has asked to be shown the issue. The presenter is then able to show us on his or her screen the process they went through and where they got stuck. Recent examples include how to share access in ClickUp or how to find something in Gmail. It's far more easy to understand a problem when it is visualized then it is when described.

Another application of Screen Sharing is for sales calls. Most salespeople will provide an outline of how their services or tools can benefit a new client. But it's an entirely new level to actually show clients inside your tool or walk them through what services you can provide them. We've found new clients love this as it actually shows them what we can and will be doing for them.

Video / Screen Recording & Screen Capture

Video recording tools allow you to record video of your screen and voice over audio. The main difference to Screen Sharing (discussed in the previous section) is that video recording is not for viewing in real time, it can be saved and viewed later. Video editing usually includes editing and sharing capabilities. In my opinion Screen Recording is one of the most underutilized collaboration tools. It is a great opportunity for your organization and a huge timesaver once you incorporate it into your workflow.

There is a spectrum when it comes to video recording tools. There is professional software for people who are looking to make lengthy video courses and professional presentations. On the lower end of the spectrum there exist cheaper, no frills options designed for creating quick shareable tutorials and internal team instructions.

Professional Screen Recording Tools

The most popular tool in the professional category is [Camtasia by TechSmith](). It is a professional level tool that comes with powerful editing features. Camtasia allows you to do things like layer audio and video tracks as well as annotations. All sorts of effects can be added in like zoom in and fade away. Video and audio can be edited to improve quality. A full list of features can be found on the [TechSmith website](). The screenshot below shows the Camtasia interface. You can see multiple video and annotation tracks along the bottom of the screen and editing features and effects in the left sidebar.

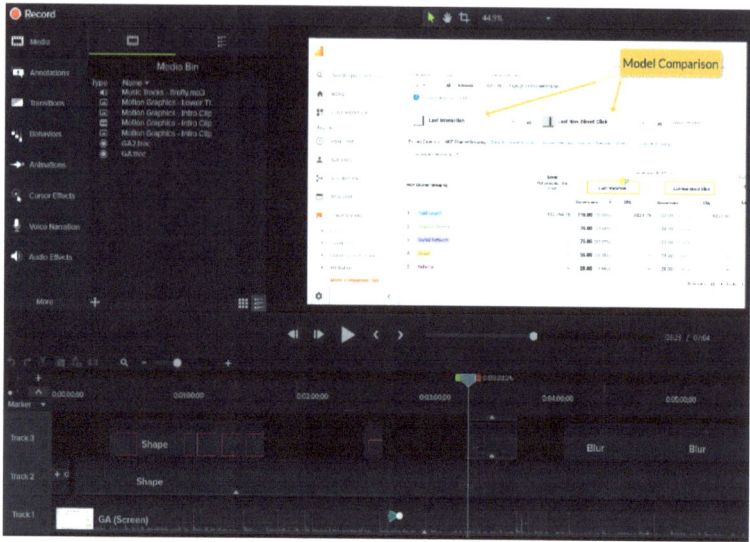

Lightweight Screen Recording Tools

For running remote teams, an easier and cheaper option is more lightweight software like useloom. Useloom is free software that allows you to quickly and easily record your screen and voice over audio. It comes with basic editing features compared to Camtasia but for the purposes of creating quick demonstration videos it has everything you need and is easier to work with. Loom can also be run as a browser extension in Chrome, once inside your Chrome browser you can start recording what's on your screen with the click of a button. Loom has detailed instructions as to how to install and use their browser extension for chrome here

Possibly the best feature of Loom is that when you finish recording your video is automatically uploaded to your Loom account in the cloud and you are provided a link. You can then quickly share this link with whoever you want to view the video. Furthermore you can then track if the video was viewed and how many times. Below is a screenshot showing my recording library in Loom which I can easily access and share.

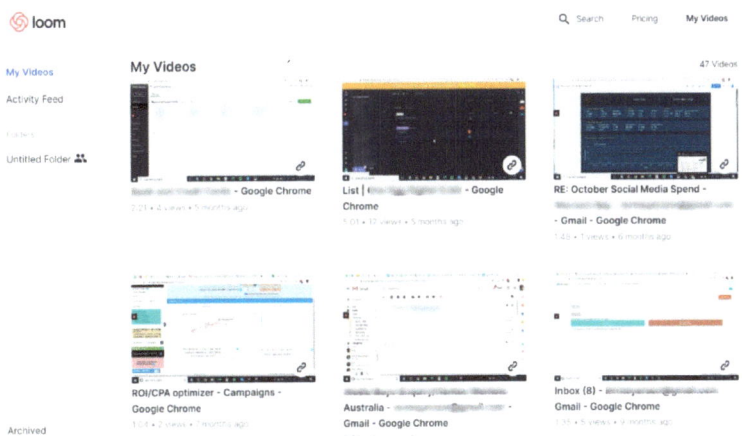

We have been long term users of loom and we have found that it has saved us a lot of time and increased accuracy and efficiency. Often you sit down and start writing an email to describe something, but then realize you could just record a quick video of your screen. We also have a database of videos that we have already recorded showing how certain repetitive tasks are done. The same applies for client recordings. This can be a better option than screen share, since it can be recorded and viewed at more convenient times. This shows clients work that has actually been done or uncovers issues for them that they can see for themselves and share with colleagues.

Screen Recording in ClickUp

Recently ClickUp, our project management tool added screen recording as a tool as well. This has been great for us, as we can record a screen record from inside a task, with the click of a button. It also allows us to minimize the number of different applications we use. Another reason we recommend ClickUp.

Screen Capture Tools

Windows comes out of the box with 'Snip and Sketch'. This is a fairly basic tool, but for most of your needs will be sufficient. It allows you to capture what's on your screen and draw over the screen highlighting certain things.

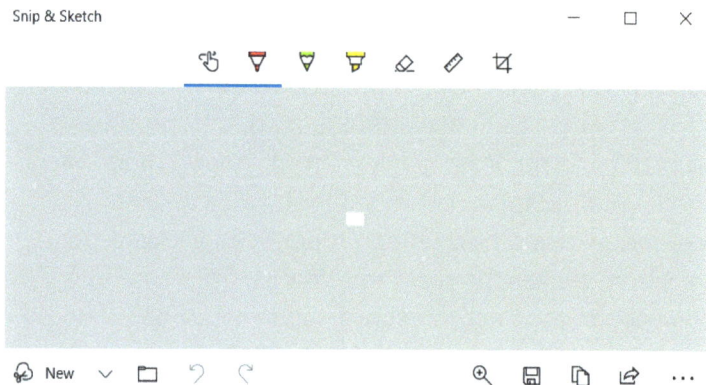

There are many tools you can use for Screen Capture. The one I use again comes out of ClickUp. It has some great features that Snip & Sketch doesn't include. Most of the screenshots in this article have been taken using the ClickUp Screen Capture, which allows me to blur parts of the image and create colored boxes to highlight and number elements.

Collaborative Documents

Collaborative documents are applications that allow multiple users to edit documents in real time. Many organizations are not up to date with this method of working. Employees are still working on documents on their local PC's, saving files locally and then emailing these documents as attachments to other team members. This is a tedious process and only works if there is one person at a time working on the document. As soon as multiple people need to work on a document, collaborating becomes tedious and slow with overlapping edits and mistakes being made. It can get messy. Collaborative documents solve this by having the document hosted in the Cloud allowing access for multiple users with edits made in real time. Edits are not overlapped, each user can work and see other users working in real time.

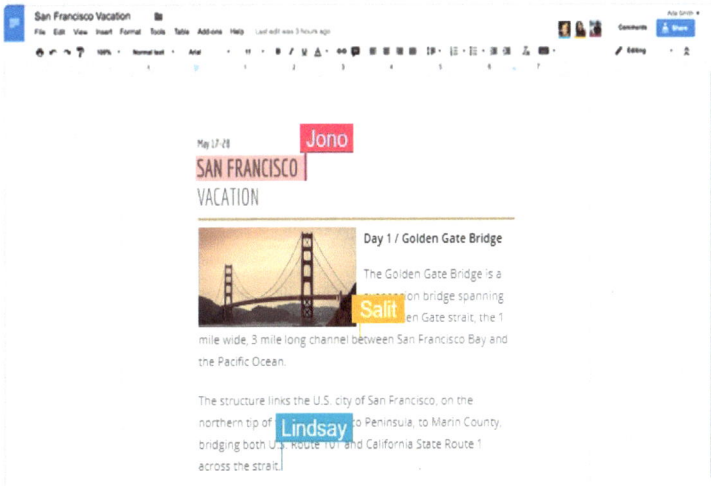

Commenting and Notifications

Commenting is another great feature of collaborative documents. Within the document one user can highlight and comment on an element such as a sentence or an image which anyone in the document can see. A member of the team can also be tagged and/or assigned to a comment, meaning they will be notified and assigned to take action on the comment. As you can see in the screenshot example below:

Collaborative Documents have come a long way, I can recall 10 years ago using Zoho Sheets. They were a frontrunner in this technology and while it worked, it was clunky and slow. The sheets would time out often and not load properly. Today it's a different story all together and these tools work as smoothly as if you were working offline.

Microsoft Office vs Google Docs

There are a number of providers available today but Microsoft & Google are the two you should be looking at. It's a hotly contested area as to which one is better. Microsoft was slower to move online, but now has full capabilities in browser based documents. They both offer word processing, spreadsheets, PowerPoint/slides as well as other document types.

Google is our tool of choice mostly because we are heavily integrated into G Suite which integrates seamlessly between Google products. Also because Google offers very high quality products for free. Google Docs is heavily integrated with Google Drive which allows documents to be automatically saved to drive. Therefore if you are using Google Docs it makes the most sense to use Google Drive as well. At the end of the day your choice will most likely come down to which ecosystem you find yourself in.

Templates and Add-ons

Both Google and Microsoft offer a large range of templates and add-ons for their products. Add-ons are like apps that you can integrate into the documents. This is usually for more advanced users but every now and again you might need this for a certain project. You can do things like add font packages, new chart styles or new formulas for novel calculations. You can even import data like share prices from other sources. Because these documents are in the Cloud they can link to real time data and third party developers that are also Cloud hosted.

Another great feature of online documents is the ability to link data between 2 documents. In the past you would have to save them in the same folder, but now you can just add a link in one to the other.

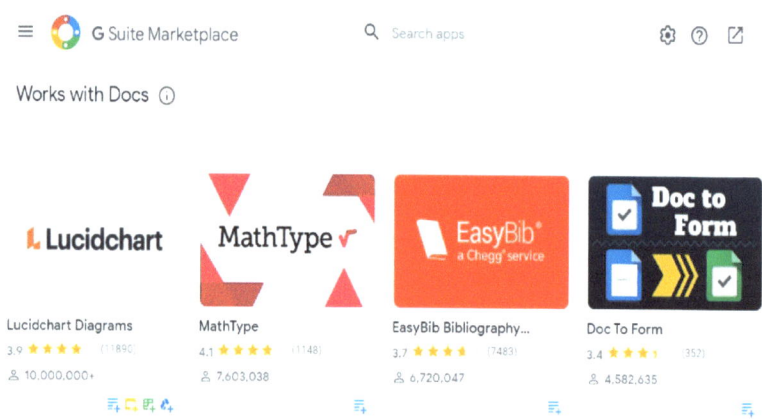

Google Doc's has a huge 3rd party add-on marketplace.

Sharing and Privacy

Sharing and privacy is a central issue with online collaborative tools. Google has invested in features allowing you to maintain maximum control. Access to users can be restricted entirely, or users can be allowed to view, comment or edit along with you. Documents can be restricted to certain email addresses or anyone given access via a link. Every scenario has been considered, from a control perspective as long as you are on top of these settings your documents will be secure.

The below screenshot shows the sharing settings for a Google Doc. I've highlighted the areas which show you 1. Sharing the document via link, 2. Which users have access and what level of access they have and the ability to invite specific users via email, 3. Security features prevent users from copying, downloading or adding new users.

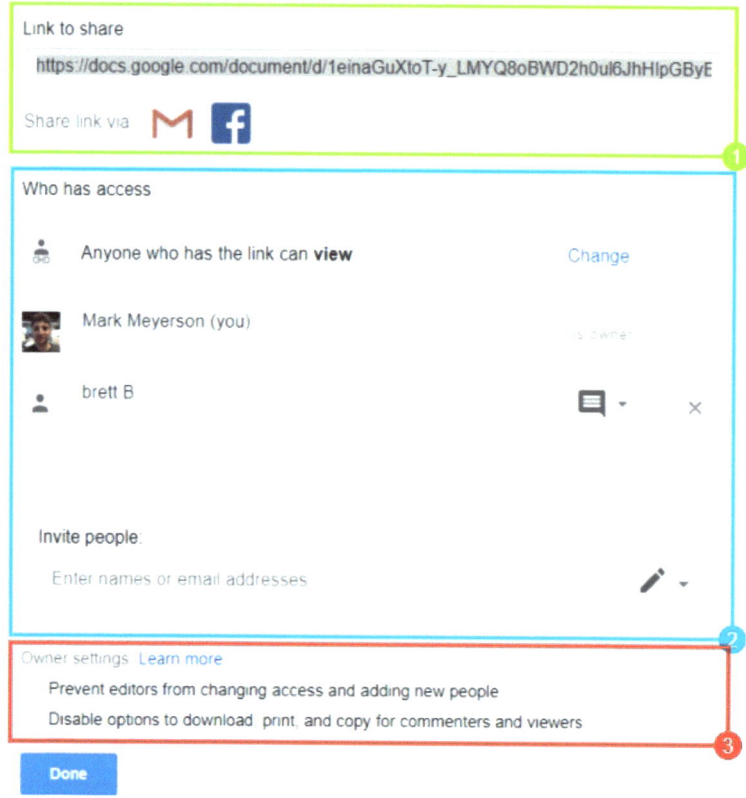

The other issue to be aware of (many are not) is that tech companies like Google may crawl your content like they crawl your Gmail account. This is a computer algorithm that reads and collects information in these documents for purposes like improving advertising. This is a broader discussion that we will not go into, but it's important to be aware of this and why the product is given away for free. In some sense, the user becomes the product.

Drive Sharing

Shared drives is a general term for file hosting, sharing and storage platforms, not to be confused with decentralized online file sharing platforms like BitTorrent (many of which are illegal). The concept of a shared drive is to move from a localized drive or folder that sits on your personal computer to one that is located in the cloud and is accessible to anyone on your team. This is beneficial for a number of reasons

Save Work in a Shared Location

Shared Drives allow team members to save work in a shared location so all members of the team can find documents in them. Locally saved documents and files can cause overlap and confusion. Shared drives solve this issue by providing a unique centralized location accessible to anyone on your team or working with your team.

Share Information and Documents

Shared drives provide the ability to share information. Since the drive is located in the Cloud, documents saved on the drive are already uploaded to the web. Most shared drive platforms allow users to share documents in these drives via a link, which effectively makes them file sharing services. Some services like wetransfer.com are designed around this purpose.

Security and Storage Considerations

Another important consideration to move to file sharing for your business is for Security & Storage. Both Dropbox and Google Drive allow users to upload files to their shared drives and then remove them from local drives. This saves space on your local machine, but the real value of this is security. User files are saved in a secure location online with tight control over user access. This is safer than saving files on a local machine which can be lost, stolen or damaged.

Shared drives come as a natural extension to collaborative documents (discussed in the above section). Once you collaborate and work on a document you need a space to save them. This is where software like Google Drive shines because it automatically saves your shared documents in your shared drive. This all happens seamlessly without any setup.

Dropbox and Google Drive

The two most widely used services in this space are Dropbox & Google Drive. Our business started out using Dropbox, being the most widely used at the time, but eventually we moved over to Google Drive since its capabilities are just as good and we were already enmeshed in the Google ecosystem, which includes Google Drive for free.

Wiki

A Wiki is a type of website that is collaboratively edited and updated by users usually used for gathering and storing knowledge. Building a Wiki for your company is a good idea whether your team is remote or local, but for remote teams it is especially useful. Wiki's are a great way to retain business knowledge in a centralized location and ensure processes are being followed and maintained.

The concept is to have a website or some kind of hosted document structure where you collect information that is important to your company and your processes. This Wiki can be collaboratively added to by all members of the company and can be constantly updated.

Benefits of A Wiki

Many companies will already have a shared document structure, using a shared drive (as discussed above). These documents probably contain information that the business needs to run. A Wiki makes this process more dynamic and user friendly, the key benefits are:

- Structure and easy navigation through interlinking within the structure.
- Searchability
- Collaborative editing tools - after an edit is made, it can go through an approval process.
- Live updates as to member changes
- Security: control of access to users

Different Ways of Using A Wiki

What your team uses the Wiki for will be different based on the business type. In our business we use a Wiki and it contains the following key sections:
- Members: a profile of each staff member, including their contact details.
- Onboarding: an outline for new members with links to sections they need to review when coming into the business.
- Client Profile: A background to each client, with information regarding clients files and project management items.
- Services Section: For each service we have an overview of the service and a subdirectory of best practice detailing how to perform those functions and processes.
- Admin: information on how to do repetitive internal tasks in the company like tracking time.

Wiki Software Providers

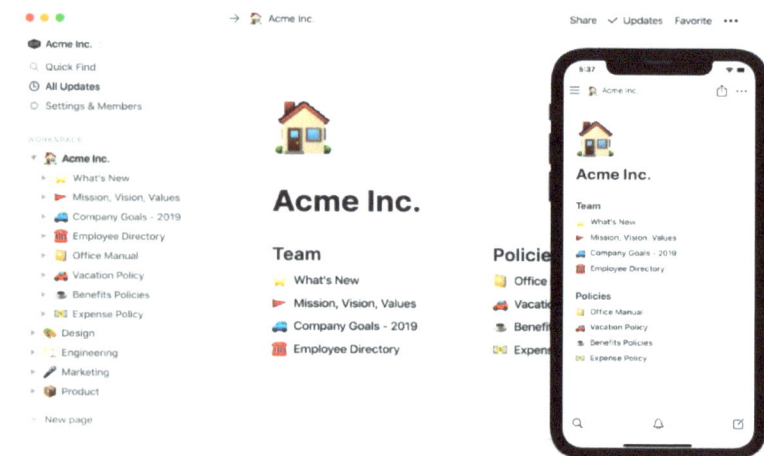

Wiki Interface in the Notion App

There are a number of great providers for Wiki Software. Confluence by Atlassian is widely used by software development companies. Confluence can be hosted on an intranet for companies concerned with security. There are a number of options for smaller business working remotely as well such as Tettra & Notion

Password Management

We've discussed security a number of times already throughout this guide because remote teams need to be especially diligent keeping information safe. Password management software is not only convenient, but also important for keeping passwords secure and in the right team members hands.

Password Chaos Is Growing

The number of passwords we deal with is growing. It's impossible to simply remember them all, which leads to users storing passwords on notepads or spreadsheets which is both inconvenient and insecure. It can be frustrating to have to look up passwords every time you log into a service. It also becomes impossible to track who was given which passwords and which ones need to be updated. This is especially problematic when members leave the team or new members join.

Solution: Centralized Password Management and Team Access Control

Password Management tools solve these problems. When you sign up to a password management tool you are asked to create one master password which is used to access a vault which stores all other passwords securely in a central location. Within this location passwords can be shared with other team members. You can control who has access to which password. Below is a screenshot of my LastPass vault which categorizes passwords, I can enter each item, update it and control who has access.

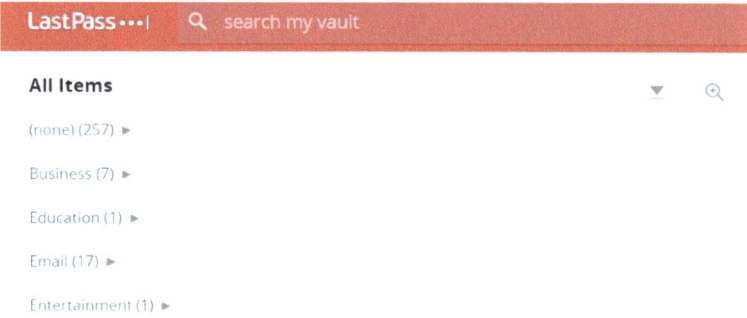

Time Saving and Convenience

Another great feature of password managers like LastPass is the autofill fields. LastPass has a browser extension that detects on a website when a user/pass is required and is able to autofill these fields for fast access. The below screenshot shows what happens when I navigate to my WordPress website login page in my browser. The LastPass extension detects the login fields and suggests possible user/pass options for me to autofill.

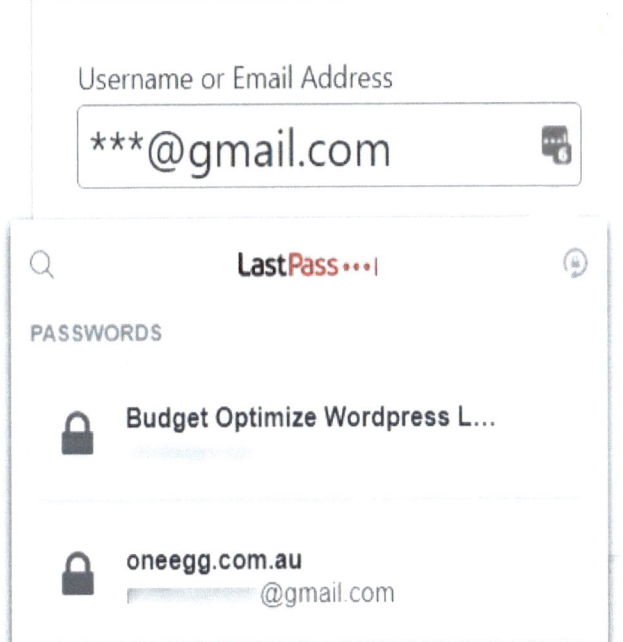

There are a number of great tools on the market today, [LastPass](#) and [1password](#) are the ones we are familiar with and both offer great low cost features.

Time Tracking

When you're not in the office working together, it's difficult to get a sense of how much time your team is spending on different projects and this lack of visibility can be frustrating for managers. Time tracking tools allow project managers to effectively manage time and ensure projects are on track.

Within these tools, managers are able to allocate time estimates at the beginning of a project. Team members are then able to update time as they work through the project and the project can be monitored to ensure it is on track and not going overtime.

Top Solutions: Toggl and Harvest

We recommend using either [Toggl](#) or [Harvest](#). Both of these tools have great time tracking capabilities that are easy for your team to get started on straight away. We decided to use Toggl as we found the mix of features best for our business, however both tools are good options.

The below screenshot shows the reporting interface in Toggl allowing project managers to easily see current time tracked per project.

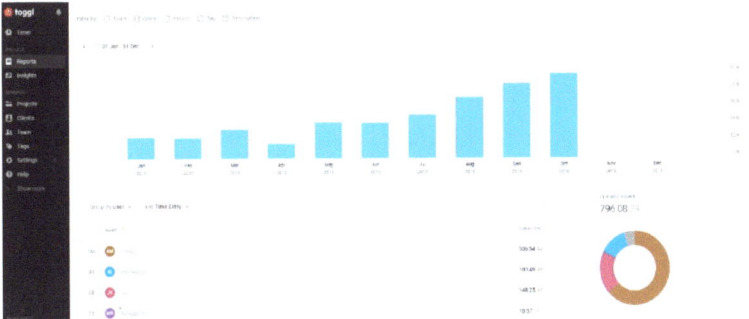

Integrations

An important consideration for time tracking is integration with other apps. You will likely want your time tracking data to be pulled into other tools that you use such as your project management tool and your accounting software. Toggl and Harvest both integrate with a number of project management tools allowing you to sync the data across. We are using ClickUp for project management, which has its own inbuilt time management tool. This is ideal since it means we can set up a project once in ClickUp and track time against it. Rather than setup projects in two different locations and integrate between them.

Harvest allows users to track billable time and then automatically integrate this into invoices. Harvest is able to generate its own invoices or integrate time data into a number of accounting software platforms like Xero or QBO.

Turn your hours into invoices.

Automatically pull the billable time and expenses you've tracked into invoices. Want more control over what you charge your client? No problem! Manually create a free-form invoice.

Avoid Being Overly Invasive and Micromanaging

It's important to tread carefully here. In my experience as both employee and employer using time management software, the way you use these tools can positively or negatively affect your team. When implementing this process at first, employees can feel like they are being micromanaged or that the time they are spending on tasks is coming into question.

Some tools like Time Doctor are overly invasive. It has a feature that takes screenshots of users screens at random intervals and then sends these screenshots back to managers - read about this here. There are also features which prevent the use of certain websites and social media or track time spent on these platforms. If you are using this for personal reasons to track your own performance, this is one thing, but for teams I think this is over intrusive. Time tracking for teams should be used only to track project time and ensure allocated time is not being exceeded.

Reporting

For remote teams it's important to have visibility over progress and results. In the office it's easy enough to walk by a colleague, have a chat and get a sense of how teams are performing and projects progressing. For remote teams having a reporting system is important and reporting can provide structure and transparency.

Internal and External Reporting

The kind of reporting you need heavily depends on what industry you are in. As an example, for our industry, marketing, we recommend having two types of reports. The first is an internal progress report and the second is a client report focused on client KPI's.

For the first report, we have an internal team report showing how each team member is progressing. ClickUp's project management tool provides a dashboard showing progress and an aggregate score for each team member. We can also see how many overdue tasks each team member has.

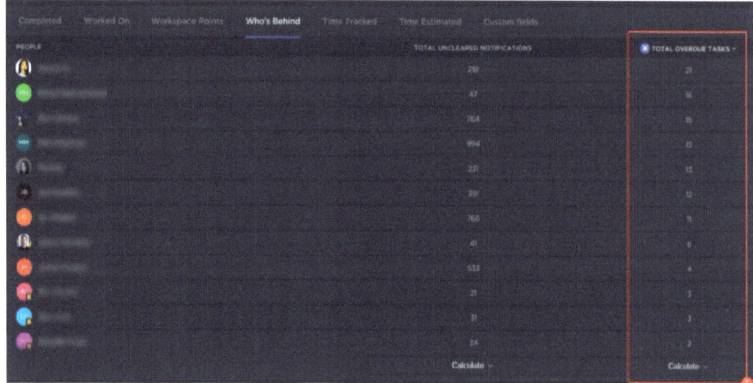

The above ClickUp report dashboard shows uncleared notifications and overdue tasks for each team member.

Client Reporting

For client KPI reporting, we use digital dashboarding technology called Google Data Studio which is accessible online and updates in real time. This tool is able to integrate directly with a number of API's and data sources including Google Sheets (Spreadsheets). Data Studio will import the data and convert it into graphs and tables which is far easier to understand and also allows the user to adjust it on the front end. Clients will appreciate the transparency and ability to access their own performance data. Datastudiotemplates.com offers a number of prebuilt templates and use cases you can explore.

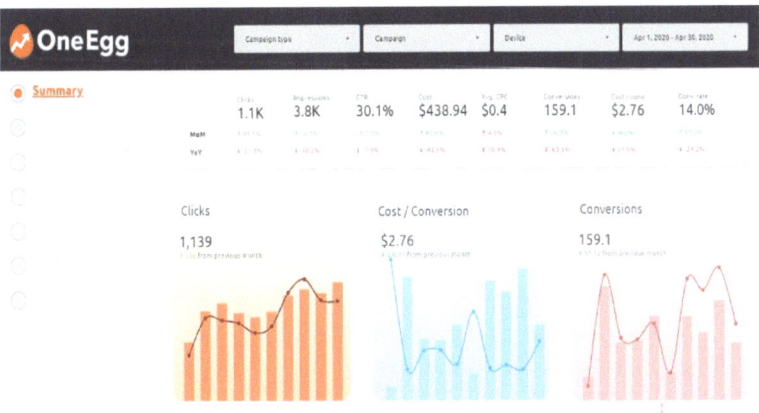

See an example Data Studio template in action:
oneegg.com.au/data-driven/data-studio/

Document Tracking / Electronic Agreements

Document tracking is mostly used for digital agreements and contracts such as proposals. The process of sending and tracking these documents can be a tedious part of doing business. Digital applications make this easier and more efficient by allowing you to easily create agreements, send them off, track and procure signatures.

Every Business is Doing Sales

This category is geared towards sales teams and not necessarily team collaboration. Yet, it is still a good example of how you can better streamline processes when working remotely and since every business is doing some form of sales, it is an important aspect to cover.

The Benefits of Document Tracking

The benefits of document tracking applications are many. Proposals built via these apps look more professional than something hacked together in Microsoft Word and sending a beautiful looking proposal is going to increase conversion rates.

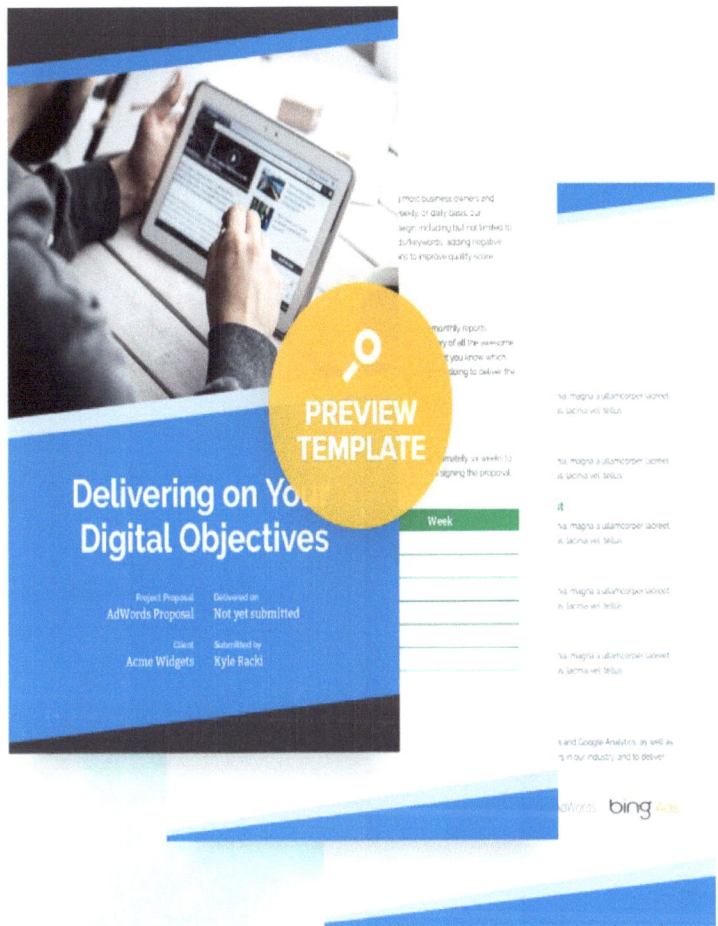

An example template from proposify.com.

These apps allow you to track the complete sales process and pick up on any issues. You can see if the proposal arrived and if it was opened and read which can help you understand why a prospect might have delayed signing it. The software also stores proposals and provides analytics on conversion rate, essentially streamlining the whole process.

Key players in this area include: DocuSign, Proposify & Better Proposals. I would suggest using software like this if you spend a lot of time on sales and are looking to make your sales process more efficient.

Health and Wellbeing

The health and wellbeing of your team is no small matter. A company has a duty of care towards its employees which includes abiding by relevant health and safety laws. However, I believe that companies should go beyond and also promote the wellbeing of their employees. Employees have the right to decide how healthy they want to be of course, but companies should be there to support healthy choices.

Happy and Healthy Employees is Good for Business

What's good for employees is also good for the team and company as a whole. When employees are healthier and fitter they will feel better about themselves and also work better and contribute more to the team as a whole. We know that fitter, healthier and happier employees bring a myriad of benefits including increased productivity. The [ACT Government's healthier work guide](#) is a good starting place to find more information on these benefits and how to promote these practices.

Studies suggest that when teams work physically close together they are motivated by each other and can gain a natural health benefit. In [this study](#) in 2010, they found that the perceived fitness level of other others makes you exercise harder. This other [study in 2016](#) showed that we tend to lose more weight if we spend time with fitter people. Therefore it's important for us to try and find ways to promote health with remote teams as well where we are physically apart from the rest of our team.

Suggestions to Improve Health and Well Being in Remote Businesses

Here are suggestions we've found to help remote teams improve their health and wellbeing:

Insist on schedule: This can be challenging with international teams but it's important to insist that employees stick to a regular shift that overlaps with other team members. This doesn't have to be 9 to 5, but should be consistent. Working too many hours will do more harm than good in the long term.

Fitness Perks: A number of businesses provide gym membership as a perk. I'm not convinced this is the best idea, as it is not a strong motivator. When someone pays for gym from their own pocket they will be more motivated to attend.

Workout Apps: Short workout apps like the [7 minute workout](#) are a great way to get started keeping healthy while working at home. Businesses should encourage this and provide time for it.

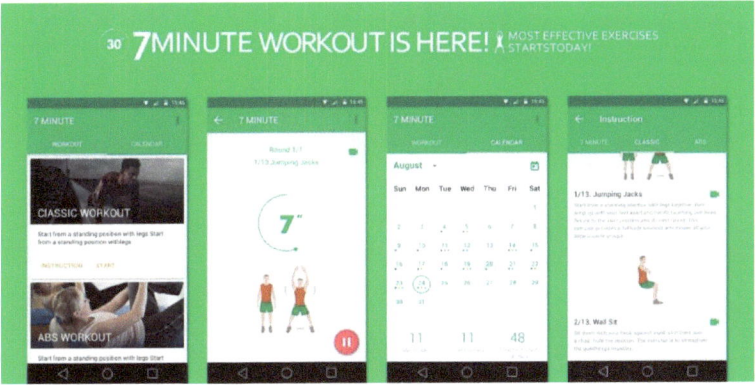

Fitbit fitness app: An interesting approach is to provide each person on the team with a Fitbit fitness tracker. The Fitbit app allows users to invite friends to participate in challenges such as daily steps or runs. This can be a fun activity to challenge your colleagues and team to. You could even import each person's data and create a dashboard. (Make sure your team is comfortable participating in this first). Fitbit also has a [corporate wellness program](#) that you can subscribe to.

Standup desks: Having a good workspace is crucial and just because your staff are not in the office doesn't mean they shouldn't be set up well. Standup desks are an easy way to promote wellness and get more blood flow happening during work. We encourage all meetings to be taken standing up. I personally find I am more aware and focused in meetings when I am standing up or pacing back and forth. Meetings are a good time to be up on your feet.

Indoor greenery: One of the easiest ways to promote health is indoor greenery. [Studies have shown](#) that indoor plants improve air quality and boost mood, productivity concentration, creativity and reduce stress.

Final Words

Running a business remotely is vastly different then working with a local team. There are many things that we take for granted when we work physically close together. Businesses that don't realize this will eventually become overwhelmed and not be able to function effectively in a remote environment.

The benefits that come with having a physically close team are important aspects of work and there are many ways we can still incorporate these features into a remote working environment. We have discussed a number of these including processes, tools and applications as well as wellbeing and health.

Running a remote team means focusing heavily on efficiency and still being able to work effectively with less day to day contact and even across time zones. Remote teams force us to build in better processes and efficiencies that will actually improve local teams as well. Whether you run a local or remote team there are always ways we can improve processes, tools and the way we work in general.

www.ingramcontent.com/pod-product-compliance
Lightning Source LLC
Chambersburg PA
CBHW040326220526
45473CB00009B/2586